CW00523984

Prayers *for* Families

David Adam
Rupert Bristow
Nick Fawcett
Gerald O'Mahony
Susan Sayers
Ray Simpson

Compiled by Sue Cowper

www.kevinmayhew.com

Prayers compiled from:

1000 Prayers for Public Worship – David Adam
Prayers for Inclusion and Diversity – Rupert Bristow
2000 Prayers for Public Worship – Nick Fawcett
Prayers for All Seasons – Nick Fawcett
Prayers for All Seasons 2 – Nick Fawcett
A Thousand and One Prayers – Gerald O'Mahony
1500 Prayers for Public Worship – Susan Sayers
His Complete Celtic Prayers – Ray Simpson

 KM PUBLISHING

First published in Great Britain in 2013 by Kevin Mayhew Ltd
Buxhall, Stowmarket, Suffolk IP14 3BW
Tel: +44 (0) 1449 737978 Fax: +44 (0) 1449 737834
E-mail: info@kevinmayhewltd.com

www.kevinmayhew.com

© Copyright 2013 David Adam, Rupert Bristow, Nick Fawcett,
Gerald O'Mahony, Susan Sayers and Ray Simpson.

The right of David Adam, Rupert Bristow, Nick Fawcett, Gerald O'Mahony,
Susan Sayers and Ray Simpson to be identified as the authors of this work
has been asserted by them in accordance with the Copyright, Designs and
Patents Act 1988.

All rights reserved. No part of this publication may be reproduced, stored in
a retrieval system, or transmitted, in any form or by any means, electronic,
mechanical, photocopying, recording, or otherwise, without the prior written
permission of the publisher.

9 8 7 6 5 4 3 2 1 0

ISBN 978 1 84867 659 6
Catalogue No. 1501407

Cover design by Rob Mortonson
© Images used under licence from Shutterstock Inc.
Typeset by Richard Weaver

Printed and bound in Great Britain

About the authors

DAVID ADAM was the Vicar of Lindisfarne, off the Northumbrian coast, for thirteen years until he retired in March 2003. His work involved ministering to thousands of pilgrims and other visitors. He is the author of many inspiring books on spirituality and prayer, and his Celtic writings have rekindled a keen interest in our Christian heritage.

RUPERT BRISTOW was Director of Education for Canterbury Diocese and a governor of Canterbury Christ Church University from 1995 until his retirement in 2008 and is active as a Reader in Trinity Benefice, Folkestone. He has worked in education – in schools, universities and administration – at home and overseas. He has also been a specialist adviser to a House of Commons select committee, edited and written for various educational publications and chaired Kent SACRE (Standing Advisory Council for Religious Education). He is an Honorary Fellow of Canterbury Christ Church University.

NICK FAWCETT was brought up in Southend-on-Sea, Essex, and trained for the Baptist ministry at Bristol and Oxford, before serving churches in Lancashire and Cheltenham. He subsequently spent three years as a chaplain with the Christian movement Toc H, before focusing on writing and editing, which he continues with today, despite wrestling with cancer. He lives with his wife, Deborah, and two children – Samuel and Kate – in Wellington, Somerset, worshipping at the local Anglican church. A keen walker, he delights in the beauty of the Somerset and Devon countryside around his home, his numerous books owing much to the inspiration he unfailingly finds there.

GERALD O'MAHONY was born in Wigan, Lancashire. He joined the Society of Jesus (the Jesuits) at the age of 18, and was ordained priest aged 30. Gerald was a school teacher for four years, before being invited to join the team of advisers in religious education for the Archdiocese of Liverpool. Ten years on he joined another team, as retreat giver and writer in Loyola Hall Jesuit Spirituality Centre, Rainhill, near Liverpool, where he has lived and worked happily ever since. He is the author of twenty-four books, many of which have been published by Kevin Mayhew.

SUSAN SAYERS is the author of many popular resource books for the church. Through the conferences and workshops she is invited to lead, she has been privileged to share in the worship of many different traditions and cultures. A teacher by profession, she was ordained a priest in the Anglican Church and, before her retirement, her work was divided between the parish of Westcliff-on-Sea, the local women's prison, writing, training days and retreats.

RAY SIMPSON is a Celtic new monastic for tomorrow's world, a lecturer, consultant, liturgist, and author of some 30 books. He is the founding guardian of the international Community of Aidan and Hilda and the pioneer of its e-studies programmes. He is an ordained member of the Christian church and lives on the Holy Island of Lindisfarne. His website is www.raysimpson.org

Contents

	Prayer No.
Weddings	1-15
Marriage and Renewal of Vows	16-28
Mothering Sunday	29-42
Father's Day	43-52
Parents	53-65
Children	66-107
Children's Prayers	108-129
Homes and Families	130-199
Families in Need	200-230

Weddings

1   Living God,
we praise you for this day of joy and celebration,
love and commitment,
nostalgia and anticipation.
For all that this day means,
we thank you.

We thank you for all A and C have shared,
and all they will share –
for the happiness they have found in each other,
and their desire today before us and you
to bear witness to that happiness.
For all that this day means,
we thank you.

We thank you for the love this service speaks of –
the love A and C have for each other,
the love of family and friends,
the love you have for us.
For all that this day means,
we thank you.

Living God,
open our hearts, we pray, to all you would say to us.
May this be a day for A and C to remember with gratitude,
the first of many days and many years of lasting fulfilment.
And may this for us all be a day
when we recognise more clearly
the greatness of your love,
and in glad thanksgiving make our response.
For all that this day means,
we thank you,
in the name of Christ we pray.   *Nick Fawcett*

2   God of love,
we come together on this special day
to give you thanks,
to celebrate,
and to worship.
Gracious God,
hear our prayer.

We come remembering everything
that has made this day possible –
the love that has surrounded A and C since their birth,
the experiences that have shaped their characters,
the events that have brought them together
and cemented their relationship.
Gracious God,
hear our prayer.

We come looking forward to everything the future holds –
the joys A and C will share,
the dreams they will work to fulfil,
the love that will continue to grow.
Gracious God,
hear our prayer.

We come rejoicing in everything this present moment has
to offer –
the reunion of family and friends,
the fun, laughter and happiness we share,
the joining together before you of husband and wife.
Gracious God,
hear our prayer.

God of love,
this is a precious day –
a time for thanksgiving, celebration, and worship.
Accept our praise for everything you have done,
and everything we are privileged to witness today.
And grant your blessing on all the future holds,
so that all we hope for and more besides
may be realised over the years to come.
Gracious God,
hear our prayer,
through Jesus Christ our Lord.   *Nick Fawcett*

3 Gracious God,
we are here to celebrate,
to rejoice and give thanks.
We come, not just to enjoy a special occasion,
but to seek your blessing upon a continuing journey,

a lifetime of exploration and discovery
in which we pray that love
will grow, flourish and blossom.
Meet with us now.
Be with us always.

We are here to witness an act of commitment,
a mutual pledging of vows,
a consecration of two lives woven into one relationship.
Meet with us now.
Be with us always.

We are here to praise you for the gift of love,
to thank you for the joy A and C have found in each other,
and to commit the future into your hands.
Meet with us now.
Be with us always.

Gracious God,
draw near to us in this service,
draw near to A and C,
and may your sovereign love enfold us all,
this day and for evermore.
Meet with us now.
Be with us always.
Through Jesus Christ our Lord.   *Nick Fawcett*

4   Loving God,
    we thank you for this special day –
    this day of rejoicing, celebration, expectation
    and new beginnings.
    Lord of love,
    hear our prayer.

    We thank you for this couple –
    all they mean to us,
    all they mean to each other,
    and all they mean to you.
    Lord of love,
    hear our prayer.

We thank you for bringing them together,
for the love they share,
and the life they look forward to.
Lord of love,
hear our prayer.

Enrich both them and us through being here today.
May the making of vows,
the exchanging of rings,
the reading of your word,
and the offering of our worship,
speak powerfully of the gift of human love,
and more powerfully still of your eternal love
that unfailingly encircles us.
Lord of love,
hear our prayer.

Loving God,
grant your blessing upon A and C,
so that in everything the future holds,
for better or for worse,
for richer for poorer,
in sickness and in health,
they may continue to cherish each other,
and their love continue to grow.
Grant that the closeness they feel now
may be just as real, as sure, and as special
tomorrow and in the years to come as it is today.
Lord of love,
hear our prayer,
in the name of Christ.   *Nick Fawcett*

5   Living God,
    there is so much to enjoy in this day,
    not simply this service now, central though it is,
    but everything else that is part of this occasion:
    the giving and receiving of gifts,
    the taking of photographs,
    the making of speeches,
    the fun of the reception,

the excitement of family and friends,
the prospect of time away on honeymoon –
so much happiness,
so much laughter,
so much to celebrate.
And we thank you for it all with glad and joyful hearts.
Lord, in your love,
hear our prayer.

But we pray that through it all
you will save us from losing sight
of what this day is really all about –
your gift of love;
and not just love in the sentimental way we use that word,
but the way you understand it:
a love that is patient and kind,
never insisting on its own way,
nor arrogant, rude, irritable or resentful,
but rejoicing in truth,
bearing all things,
believing all things,
hoping all things,
enduring all things.
Lord, in your love,
hear our prayer.

Living God,
help us to enjoy this day,
celebrating every part of it enthusiastically
as your gift to us.
But help us also to remember that without love at its heart
this day would be nothing.
And so grant your blessing upon A and C,
and upon each of us in our own relationships,
so that whatever we may face
our love may continue to grow,
this day and always.
Lord, in your love,
hear our prayer,
in the name of Jesus Christ our Lord.   *Nick Fawcett*

6   Sovereign God,
this is a day of love –
a time of joining together,
exchanging vows,
uniting two lives as one.
For all that this day means,
receive our praise.

This is a day of joy –
an occasion of celebration,
laughter,
and thanksgiving.
For all that this day means,
receive our praise.

This is a day for reminiscing –
for remembering everything A and C have meant
to their loved ones over the years,
for looking back to the times we have shared with them,
and for recalling how their love for each other has grown
since they first met.
For all that this day means,
receive our praise.

This is a day for anticipation –
for looking forward to everything the future holds,
for sharing in A and C's excitement as they plan ahead,
and for rejoicing in this new chapter in their lives.
For all that this day means,
receive our praise.

This is a day for worship –
for recognising your presence here among us,
acknowledging your goodness
and asking your blessing on A and C
in the years ahead.
For all that this day means,
receive our praise.

Sovereign God,
we thank you for this special day –
put your hand upon it.

We thank you for this special couple –
put your hand on them.
We thank you for the opportunity
to share in this happy occasion –
put your hand on us.
Come now,
and make this time everything we want it to be,
and everything you can make it become.
For all that this day means,
receive our praise.
Through Jesus Christ our Lord.   *Nick Fawcett*

7   Gracious God,
    we thank you for A and C,
    for all they mean to each other,
    and all they mean to us.
    Loving Lord,
    gratefully we worship you.

    We thank you for the way you have brought A and
    C together,
    the times they have shared,
    and the love that has grown between them.
    And we praise you that they have reached this point
    of committing themselves to each other in marriage,
    pledging before you and this congregation
    their desire to share their lives together,
    for better, for worse,
    for richer, for poorer,
    in sickness and in health,
    till they are parted by death.
    Loving Lord,
    gratefully we worship you.

    We thank you for the joy that A and C feel at this moment,
    and the joy we share with them;
    the sense of promise and excitement
    which has touched all our lives today,
    and which we pray will continue for A and C
    in the years ahead.

Loving Lord,
gratefully we worship you.

We thank you for everything that has led up to this day –
the moment A and C first met,
the way they have grown together,
the planning and preparation behind this service
and the reception to come,
the buying of gifts and sending of cards –
everything that helps to make this day so special.
And, above all, we thank you for your guiding hand
which makes not just this day possible, but every day,
and which is always outstretched in love,
looking to draw us to your side.
Loving Lord,
gratefully we worship you.

Gracious God,
we come today with grateful hearts,
to celebrate,
to rejoice,
and to seek your blessing on the journey
which A and C are stepping out into today.
Go with them both,
and with us all,
now and for evermore.
Loving Lord,
gratefully we worship you.
In the name of Christ.   *Nick Fawcett*

Before the start of a wedding service
8 Open our eyes to your presence.
Open our ears to your call.
Open our hearts to your love.   *Ray Simpson*

After the entrance of the bride as she stands beside the groom
9 Most powerful Spirit of God,
come down upon us and subdue us.
From heaven –
where the ordinary is made glorious

and glory seems but ordinary –
bathe us with the brilliance
of your light, like dew.   *Ray Simpson*

Before the vows
10 May the Father take you
in his fragrant clasp of love,
in every up and every down of your life.   *Ray Simpson*

11 The love and affection of God be with you.
The love and affection of the angels
be with you.
The love and affection of the saints in heaven
be with you.
The love and affection of your friends on Earth
be with you,
to guard you,
to cherish you,
to bring you to your eternal fulfilment.   *Ray Simpson*

Joining hands after the vows
12 May you be bound
with unbreakable bonds of love to one another.
May you be bound
with unbreakable bonds of love to your God.
May your love for each other
reflect the love of your Maker, Saviour and Guide:
the Three of Limitless Love.   *Ray Simpson*

A bridal blessing after the vows
13 May the Father take you in his fragrant clasp of love.
May the Virgin Mary's Son guide you
through the maze of life.
May the generous Spirit release forgiving love within you.
Hour by hour, by day and by night, in joy and in failure,
may each man and each woman who is a saint in heaven
urge you on to complete your course.   *Ray Simpson*

14 God's own presence with you stay,
Jesus to shield you in the fray,
Spirit to protect you from all ill,
Trinity there guiding you still.
On sea or land, in ebb or flow,
God be with you wherever you go;
in flow or ebb, on land or sea,
God's great might your protecting be.   *Ray Simpson*

15 May you share hopes and dreams,
but also walk through hard times hand in hand.
May your love for each other keep burning bright,
but if ever it flickers low may Jesus,
the Eternal Fire Kindler, light up the fire again.
In your old age, as now when you are younger,
may you be best friends,
and give each other room to be yourselves.   *Ray Simpson*

Marriage and Renewal of Vows

16 We pray for all marriages,
for those seeking marriage partners
and those whose marriages are under strain.
We pray for all in close relationships,
that there may be mutual love and respect.   *Susan Sayers*

17 Gracious God,
we are here to celebrate your love,
and rejoice in your great faithfulness.
You have been always good to us,
always true,
always by our side,
and we praise you for it.
Receive our praise,
in the name of Christ.

Day by day you have held us close,
sharing with us in the good times and bad,
our surest and dearest friend,
and we thank you for it.
Receive our praise,
in the name of Christ.

Gracious God,
we are here to celebrate your gift of love,
the love that A and C have shared over so many years,
the faithfulness they have shown to each other –
the closeness that has grown between them.
Receive our praise,
in the name of Christ.

We are here to celebrate how you have sustained them,
through joy and sorrow,
hopes and fears,
trials and temptations,
good and bad.
Receive our praise,
in the name of Christ.

Gracious God,
we are here to celebrate,
with you,
with A and C,
and with one another.
Speak to us through the vows renewed in this service,
of the love you have for us,
and help us to pledge our love in return to you.
Receive our praise,
in the name of Christ.   *Nick Fawcett*

18   Eternal God,
we come today to celebrate the gift of love –
your love for us,
and the love of A and C for each other.
You have blessed us,
and we thank you.

We thank you that though all else may change,
though heaven and earth may pass away,
your love continues unchanging,
constant and dependable,
always the same,
always certain.
You have blessed us,
and we thank you.

We thank you for the way you have been with A and C
throughout their lives –
the way you brought them together,
the way you have guided them,
nurtured and enriched their relationship,
and blessed them and their loved ones.
You have blessed us,
and we thank you.

We thank you for their commitment to each other,
to their family,
to us,
and to Christ.
You have blessed us,
and we thank you.

Go with them now,
watch over them,
and grant them many more years
of health and happiness together,
until that day when you unite them and all your people
in your everlasting kingdom
and the joy of your unchanging presence.
You have blessed us,
and we thank you,
in the name of Christ.   *Nick Fawcett*

19   Gracious God,
we praise you for your gift of love –
that most precious of gifts which endures beyond all others,
bearing all things,
believing all things
and hoping all things.
We rejoice that it is a love such as this
which we come to celebrate today.
Receive our thanks,
and accept our worship.

We thank you for the joy that comes
from two lives truly being shared,
from two people becoming one,

each complementing and enriching the other,
each helping love to grow.
Receive our thanks,
and accept our worship.

We recall before you everything A and C have shared
across the years –
the joys and sorrows,
hopes and fears,
triumphs and disappointments,
pleasure and pain –
and we thank you that they have shared those times
together,
offering mutual support, strength and encouragement.
Receive our thanks,
and accept our worship.

We celebrate everything their love has meant to others –
the inspiration it has given,
happiness it has contributed to,
security it has provided,
and example it has offered to family and friends alike.
Receive our thanks,
and accept our worship.

We acknowledge your love which has been a constant thread
throughout their relationship –
your presence which has always been with them,
your hand upon them today,
and the assurance that you will continue to bless them
in the years ahead,
whatever life may bring.
Receive our thanks,
and accept our worship.

So now we bring you this day of celebration
and this act of recommitment,
acknowledging with gratitude the good times enjoyed,
and looking forward with expectation to the joys yet to come.
Receive our thanks,
and accept our worship.
Through Jesus Christ our Lord.   *Nick Fawcett*

Blessing at a silver, ruby, golden or diamond
wedding celebration

20 For the love we celebrate today –
the mutual commitment across the years,
the working, sharing and building together
through good times and bad,
hopes and fears,
joys and sorrows –
we give glad and heartfelt thanks.
May that love,
that bond,
that closeness
bless and enrich you as surely in the days to come
as in the years gone by,
and may God go with you,
now and always.
Nick Fawcett

(This prayer is for those who have experienced difficulties in
their marriage and who wish to remake their vows as a symbol
of their desire to start again.)

21 Living God,
you tell us that love is patient and kind,
not envious or boastful, arrogant or rude.
You say that love is not irritable or resentful,
insisting on its own way and rejoicing in wrongdoing,
but, instead, it rejoices in the truth,
bearing all things,
believing all things,
hoping all things,
enduring all things.
We confess that our love isn't always like that,
all too often falling far short of such an ideal.
It is sometimes shaken,
and, on occasions, tested to breaking point.
Yet we come today acknowledging our weakness
and asking for another chance to love as you love us.
Receive what we are,
and direct what we shall be.

We come with A and C today,
acknowledging mistakes that have been made,
errors of judgement and lack of thought –
the words that shouldn't have been spoken
and those that should but never were;
the deeds that shouldn't have been contemplated
and those we failed even to consider –
and we ask your forgiveness for them all.
Receive what we are,
and direct what we shall be.

Give to A and C the ability to start afresh –
to put the past behind them,
learning its lessons yet allowing its wounds to heal –
and help each of us in turn to learn likewise,
open to others' point of view,
ready to forgive and forget,
always looking to see the best rather than the worst.
Receive what we are
and direct what we shall be.

Living God,
we believe you are a God who makes all things new,
constantly restoring and recreating,
and so we come to share in this act of rededication,
this renewal of vows and affirming of commitment.
Move within A and C,
work within us,
and fill each one of us with your love,
in body, mind and spirit.
Receive what we are,
and direct what we shall be.
Through Jesus Christ our Lord.   *Nick Fawcett*

22   When we have buried your insight beneath falsehoods,
when we have insulated ourselves
from being vulnerable to others,
when we have been closed to your renewing of our minds,
have mercy on us.
Break through our resistance.
Open our hearts to love.   *Ray Simpson*

23   Source of our being and goal of our longing,
give us wisdom to harvest our life
and find the wholeness of memory.
We bring to you abandoned areas of our lives.
Heal our wounds, keep bright the flame.
Kindle in us the memory of love and discovery. *Ray Simpson*

24   Eternal Wisdom, firstborn of creation,
you emptied yourself of power
and became foolish for our sake.
You laboured with us on the cross
and became Wisdom's crown.
At this table we lay down our proud pretensions
and become one with you.
We pray for
the oppressed and powerless peoples of the world,
that in their powerlessness
they may discover Wisdom's Way.   *Ray Simpson*

25   Wisdom, breathing through all creation,
you planted your likeness in us.
As a mother tenderly gathers her children
you embraced a people as your own.   *Ray Simpson*

26   Heavenly Father
we offer you our praise and thanksgiving
for [number] years together;
for all the joys we have shared;
for our friends and family (especially our children [names]).
May they always know of our love for them,
and grant us wisdom in the years to come.   *Ray Simpson*

27   Forgive us
when we grumble about the married state;
when we complain we haven't enough money;
when we are quarrelsome
and won't admit we are wrong;
and when we find fault with each other.   *Ray Simpson*

28   Heavenly Father,
we offer you our souls and bodies,
our thoughts and words and deeds,
our love for one another,
our past and our future.
Unite our will in your will.
May we and our children
grow together in love and peace
all the days of our life,
through Jesus Christ our Lord.

Ray Simpson

Mothering Sunday

29   Gracious God,
as a mother loves her child so you love us.
For that great truth
we praise and thank you.
We owe our very lives to you.
You have watched over us from our birth,
tenderly nurturing us,
showering us with love.
When we have needed you, you have been there.
You have given us strength in times of need,
comfort in times of distress,
encouragement in times of despair,
guidance in times of uncertainty.
Whatever we have faced, you have been with us.

Gracious God,
we have not always appreciated your love,
all too often ignoring what you would teach us,
disobeying your instructions,
taking you for granted and wandering far from your side.
Yet through it all your love has remained constant.

Gracious God,
caring for us more than you care for yourself,
sacrificing your all for our sakes,
loving us with an unquenchable love,
you have called us all to be your children.

For that great truth
we praise and thank you,
in the name of Christ.

Nick Fawcett

30   Gracious God,
on this special day of thanksgiving
we catch a glimpse,
through a mother's love for her child,
of your love for us;
the care, dedication and devotion you show to all your
children
which makes you as much 'our Mother' as 'our Father'.
For the intensity of your love,
Lord, we praise you.

As a mother nurtures her children,
instructing,
feeding,
clothing,
guiding,
so you nurture us,
carefully leading us towards maturity.
As a mother tends her children,
comforting in times of distress,
reassuring in times of uncertainty,
encouraging in times of challenge,
nursing in times of sickness,
so you tend us,
always there to lift us up
and set us on our feet again when we fall.

As a mother protects her children,
watching over them day by day,
alert to danger,
keeping them from harm,
and ready if necessary to sacrifice herself for their sakes,
so you protect us,
your arms constantly encircling us,
your hand delivering us from evil.

Gracious God,
Mother and Father of us all,
we rejoice today in the wonder of your love
and the constancy of your care.
Gratefully we respond,
in joyful worship
and heartfelt thanksgiving.
For the intensity of your love,
Lord, we praise you.
In the name of Christ, your only Son.   *Nick Fawcett*

31   Forgive us, Lord,
for we take you for granted,
forgetting the way you hold us in your arms,
as a mother cradles her child;
the way you teach,
provide,
comfort and lead,
always there when we need you most.
Help us to respond,
not just today but every day,
in grateful and loving service.   *Nick Fawcett*

32   Gracious God,
we are reminded today
of how easily we take a mother's love for granted,
failing to express our thanks for the care we receive,
slow to demonstrate our appreciation
for the patient nurture given over so many years.
We are reminded equally of how easily we take your love
for granted,
failing to thank you for the blessings you shower upon us,
the care with which you daily surround us,
and the joy with which you fill our lives.
We have assumed that words do not need saying,
that our thankfulness can be taken as read.
We have believed love comes easily,
failing to recognise what it can sometimes cost.
We have imagined because no thanks is asked
that no thanks is necessary.

Gracious God,
help us to understand the joy we can bring
through saying thank you,
not just today but every day,
not just to our mothers but to everyone,
and not just to everyone but to you.
And help us, through the act of thanksgiving,
to recognise how much we have to be thankful for.

Nick Fawcett

33 Gracious God,
on this special day we thank you for mothers –
our own mothers and mothers everywhere.
We thank you for all they do, or once did,
all they give, or once gave,
all they mean, and will always mean.

Grant to all entrusted with the responsibility of motherhood
your wisdom,
your guidance,
your support.
We thank you that you love us as a mother loves her child –
passionately, fiercely, devotedly, wholeheartedly –
and that, like a mother, you watch over us
every moment of every day,
seeking our welfare,
concerned about our progress,
equipping us for the journey of life.
You are always there when we need you,
ready to comfort, encourage and reassure,
slow to punish and swift to bless.

Gracious God,
we call you 'our Father',
but equally you are our Mother.
Help us to learn what that means,
and to rejoice in that truth.

Nick Fawcett

34 Loving God,
we thank you for mothers –
for all they mean or have meant to us,
for the love they have shown,

and the care they have given.
We thank you for the dedication of mothers –
the sacrifices they make,
the support they offer,
the comfort they bring,
and the guidance they provide.
We thank you for the qualities of mothers –
their patience,
kindness,
concern
and understanding.
We thank you for the role of mothers,
the part they play in our lives,
our homes,
our society
and our world.
We thank you for the joy of mothers –
the pleasure,
enrichment,
laughter and fulfilment,
which raising children brings.
We thank you for time spent with mothers –
the learning,
playing,
caring and sharing,
which are part of family life.

Loving God,
we thank you for this day of saying thank you,
this opportunity to say what we so often mean to say
but so rarely do.
For mothers and motherhood,
for children and families,
we bring you this day our grateful praise.   *Nick Fawcett*

35   Loving God,
we thank you for this day –
this day of remembering,
rejoicing,
and responding.

We thank you for our homes and all we associate with them –
the joy of family life,
the debt we owe to our parents,
and especially today the love of our mothers across the years.
We thank you for the much wider family of which we are a
part –
the family of humankind,
of this fellowship,
and the Church universal.
We thank you for the love you show us –
the same love a mother feels for her child,
the same patience and understanding,
the same concern and protectiveness.

Loving God,
grant your blessing upon all mothers and all families this day;
upon the family of humankind the world over,
upon the family of your Church, here and everywhere.
And grant your special care and support
to all those deprived of a mother's love,
and all those who have not yet come to know
your love for themselves.
Lord of all,
hear our prayer,
in the name of Christ.   *Nick Fawcett*

36   Caring and compassionate God,
     speak to us today through the love shown by mothers
     of your love for us and all:
     the love that brought us into being,
     that has nurtured us across the years,
     that welcomes us here
     and that will go on reaching out,
     come what may,
     for all eternity.

     Help us, as we honour what motherhood means,
     to honour you also,
     recognising that you show the same devotion and more,
     an unswerving commitment to your children's welfare;
     and teach us, as part of your family,

to respond accordingly,
loving you in return,
expressing our gratitude,
and living as you have taught us,
through Jesus Christ our Lord.   *Nick Fawcett*

37   Gracious God,
you know what it is to love your children –
to watch over them tenderly, anxiously,
proudly, and constantly.
You know what this means,
for you have called us your children,
and you care for each of us
as deeply as a mother cares for her child.
So now we pray for those
entrusted with the responsibility of motherhood –
all those who watch over their children in the same way,
with the same feelings and intensity.

Grant to each one your wisdom, guidance, and strength.
We pray especially for single mothers –
those faced with the challenge
of raising a child or children on their own,
with no one else to share the demands or joys of parenthood.
Give to each of them patience, devotion, and dedication.

We pray for those who have lost their mothers
or have never known them,
those orphaned as children or given up for adoption,
those whose mothers have died;
all for whom this day brings pain rather than pleasure.
Grant them your comfort, your support,
and the assurance of your love always with them.

We pray finally for those who are separated from their
children –
those whose children have moved far from home,
those who have suffered a miscarriage
or been through an abortion,
those who have endured the agony of a child's death.
Give to them your help, your solace, and hope for the future.

Gracious God,
you understand what mothers face,
what they give,
what they feel.
Accept our thanks for them this day,
and grant them your special blessing.
Lord of love,
hear our prayer,
in the name of Christ.   *Nick Fawcett*

38   Gracious God,
on this Mothering Sunday we bring you our prayers
for all entrusted with the responsibility of motherhood.
We pray for mothers the world over,
recognising both the joys and demands they experience –
the privilege and pressures,
hopes and fears,
pleasure and pain that motherhood entails.
Equip them with the love, wisdom and strength they need.

We pray for single mothers,
bearing the responsibility of parenthood alone,
struggling sometimes to make ends meet,
and stigmatised by certain sections of society.
Grant them the emotional, physical and financial resources
they need.

We pray for mothers who have experienced heartbreak –
their children stillborn or seriously disabled,
injured, maimed or killed through accident or assault,
struck down by debilitating disease or terminal illness.
Comfort them in their sorrow.

We pray for those denied the joy of motherhood –
enduring the trauma of infertility,
prevented on health grounds from risking a pregnancy,
or unable to establish a relationship
into which children can be born.
Help them to come to terms with their pain.

We pray for those who foster or adopt children,
those who long to do so but who are denied the
opportunity,
and those who for various reasons
have given up their children
and who are haunted by the image of what might have been.
Grant them your strength and support.

We pray finally for those who long to discover their
natural mothers,
those who have become estranged from them,
and those whose mothers have died –
all for whom Mothering Sunday brings pain rather
than pleasure,
hurt rather than happiness.
May your love enfold them always.

Gracious God,
we pray for mothers and children everywhere.
May your blessing be upon them,
your hand guide them,
and your love enrich them all.   *Nick Fawcett*

39   Lord God,
     we thank you for our earthly opportunities for
     mothering and being mothered,
     we also remember
     the mothering of you,
     our parent God.   *Susan Sayers*

40   We pray to you, our loving parent God,
     as children in one family.
     We thank you, loving God,
     for giving us one another to enjoy,
     to laugh and cry with, to learn to live with.
     May even our conflicts and arguments be used
     in helping us to grow up in your love.   *Susan Sayers*

41 Mother, dear pearl of great price,
too often have we taken you for granted.
May the Holy Trinity protect you.
May the Three of Limitless Love renew you so that
an island shall you be in our seas,
a light shall you be in our nights,
a well shall you be in our deserts,
until heaven's arms enfold you.   *Ray Simpson*

42 Lord of waiting,
we pray for mothers as they wait to give birth.
Help them to have patience and stamina,
endurance and hope.
Relieve them of too much worry, Lord.
Save them from too much pain,
as nature takes its course,
but with a helping hand to grasp
and a Saviour Christ who understands
the meaning and purpose of waiting,
and the promise of peace after pain.   *Rupert Bristow*

Father's Day

43 Loving God,
we come on this Father's Day,
reminded that you are the Father of us all.
You have been with us from our birth,
guiding, nurturing, and sustaining us.
Father God,
we praise you.

You have taught us and brought us to maturity,
always concerned for our welfare,
constantly seeking the best for us.
Father God,
we praise you.

Whenever we have needed you, you have been there,
willing to listen and advise,
yet giving us freedom to make our own choices
and find our own way.
Father God,
we praise you.

You have called us to be your family,
a people united through your Son, Jesus Christ,
and through him you have revealed your love,
a love that reaches out to us day by day
despite our failure to love you in return.
Father God,
we praise you.

Teach us to live as your children –
to hear your voice,
obey your instruction,
and respond to your goodness.
Father God,
we praise you.

Teach us to bear your name with pride,
to share with others,
through word and deed,
the joy you have given us.
Father God,
we praise you.

And finally receive our thanks
for the fathers you have given us,
all they have meant to us,
all they have given,
and all they have done in so many ways.
Father God,
we praise you,
in the name of Christ.

Nick Fawcett

44 Sovereign God,
Creator of the heavens and the earth,
Ruler over space and time,
we praise you that we can respond to you as a Father;

that we can approach you,
not in a spirit of subservience or fear,
but as your children,
assured of your love and secure in your purpose.

We praise you that you care for us
as much as any father cares for his child
and far more besides –
your hand always there to guide and discipline,
to provide and protect,
to comfort and encourage,
to nurture and cherish.

We praise you that your love is inexhaustible –
that, however often we fail you,
however many times we may stray from your side,
you seek us out,
striving to restore the relationship we have broken,
always ready to forgive and forget.

We praise you that we are made in your image,
capable of understanding good and evil,
able to appreciate treasure in heaven
as well as the many riches of this world,
and able also to respond to your love in Christ
and so inherit your kingdom.

Sovereign God,
we come to you on this Father's Day,
giving thanks for everything that fathers mean to us,
but rejoicing above all in your fatherly care for all.
With grateful hearts, we bring you praise,
and commit ourselves again to your service.   *Nick Fawcett*

45 Loving God,
we come together on this Father's Day,
reminded not just of our earthly fathers but of you.
You tell us that all who believe in you
shall be called your children,
and you invite us to address you quite simply as 'our Father'.
For the wonder of your love,
we praise you.

We praise you that, despite all our weakness and disobedience,
you view us not as subjects,
or as servants,
but as children.
And we rejoice that you want us to see you
not as some deity remote in splendour,
nor as a jealous God demanding our homage,
but as a father, watching over us
with infinite care and tenderness.

Loving Father,
teach us not simply to say 'our Father',
but to mean it –
to recognise that you love us as deeply,
as dependably,
and as devotedly as any human father,
and infinitely more besides.
Teach us that we matter to you,
that you are concerned for our welfare,
that you delight to bless us,
that we need only to ask and you are there.
Teach us that it is because you care so much
that you instruct us,
discipline us,
and correct us.
Teach us that, however far we stray from you,
however much we may reject your love
or ignore your guidance,
still you go on reaching out,
longing to draw us close once more.

Loving God,
you are 'our Father' and we praise you.
Teach us to be your children,
in the name of Christ.

Nick Fawcett

46 Gracious God,
we thank you today for fathers and for all that they do,
their role sometimes taken for granted
and yet meaning so much.

We thank you for our own fathers –
for all they have meant to us,
everything they have contributed to our lives,
and we acknowledge, with gratitude,
the support they have offered;
the care they have shown,
the instruction they have given,
and the love they have shared.

We thank you for the privilege of fatherhood –
the wonder of sharing in the creation of a new life,
the thrill of seeing a child mature into adulthood,
the awe-inspiring responsibility of nurturing, guiding,
enabling and encouraging,
and the sheer joy of giving and receiving love,
building a relationship that will endure for a lifetime and
beyond.

Gracious God,
we thank you for fathers
and, above all, we thank you for your fatherhood,
your creation of all,
your constant nurture,
your unfailing love which delights to call us your children
and which is always looking to draw us more deeply
into the family of your people.   *Nick Fawcett*

47 Help us, Lord,
to show our love for you,
not through sophisticated language or polished prayers,
but through true commitment,
responding with childlike trust, gratitude and affection
to your fatherly care.
Teach us to open our hearts to you,
as you have so freely done to us.   *Nick Fawcett*

48 Gracious God,
on this day for remembering, acknowledging
and celebrating fathers,
help us to remember that you call us your children
and that you ask us in turn to call you 'our Father'.

Teach us what that means:
that you care about our welfare;
that you provide for our needs and protect us from danger;
that you delight to bless and cherish;
that you strive to equip us for life,
to teach, guide, support and enable.

Help us, then, as we honour the place of fathers in our lives,
or commit ourselves more fully to faithful parenthood,
also to honour you,
growing and living obediently as your children,
so that we might attain maturity in Christ
and inherit the fullness of life you offer through him.
In his name we pray.   *Nick Fawcett*

49   Gracious God,
you know the joy of fatherhood and also the pain,
for you witnessed the life and death of your Son,
and you see each day the triumphs and tragedies of us,
your children.
Lord God our Father,
reach out in love.

You experienced the delight of being a father –
as you watched Jesus grow and mature into adulthood,
as you saw him baptised in the Jordan,
as day by day he responded to your guidance,
faithful to the very last –
a beloved son with whom you were well pleased.
Yet also you experienced agony –
in the horror of the Cross,
the pain, the humiliation,
and the sorrow he endured for our sakes.
Lord God our Father,
reach out in love.

In each of us you find pleasure –
when we pursue what is good,
when we honour your commandments,
when we seek your will and respond to your guidance.

But we cause you also so much pain –
through our weakness,
our repeated disobedience,
our deafness to your call and our rejection of your love.
Lord God our Father,
reach out in love.

Gracious God,
you know the joy and the pain of fatherhood,
and so now we pray for fathers everywhere.
Help them to appreciate both the privilege
and the responsibility they bear,
and teach them to give freely of themselves
so that they may discover the happiness,
the fulfilment,
and the inexpressible rewards that fatherhood brings.
Lord God our Father,
reach out in love.

Give them wisdom, patience, and dedication,
and grant them strength to persevere
when children bring tears as well as laughter,
anxiety as well as hope,
pain as well as pleasure.
Lord God our Father,
reach out in love.

Reach out, we pray, to all fathers in such circumstances –
those who question their ability to cope,
or who fear they have failed;
those striving to offer support,
or who feel they have nothing left to give.
Lord God our Father,
reach out in love.

And finally hear our prayer for children
who on this Father's Day feel pain instead of joy –
those whose fathers have died,
those orphaned as children,
those who have been mistreated, rejected, abused,
and those from broken homes
who barely see or know their fathers.

Lord God our Father,
reach out in love,
through Jesus Christ our Lord.

Nick Fawcett

50   Father God,
we pray today for those entrusted with the responsibility
of fatherhood,
all who have the duty and privilege of raising children,
fashioning their lives,
offering a stable and loving environment in which they
can grow,
leading them along the exciting yet demanding path
to adulthood.
Grant them love, insight and devotion.

We pray for fathers whose marriage
or relationship with their partner has broken down;
separated from their children or seeing them only occasionally,
many having responsibilities for another family,
and we pray also for those
who will fill the role of stepfather.
Grant them commitment, dedication and sensitivity.

We pray for fathers with no sense of responsibility,
failing to make time for their children,
careless in offering support and guidance,
casual in providing discipline,
essentially washing their hands of their role as parents.
Grant them forgiveness, understanding
and the opportunity to make amends.

We pray for children of broken homes,
deprived of a father figure
or knowing first one, then another,
rarely able to establish a meaningful and lasting
relationship.
Grant them stability, support
and the knowledge that they are still loved.

We pray for children abused by their fathers,
emotionally scarred for life,
struggling to come to terms with their experience,
haunted by an image of fear rather than love.
Grant them healing, peace and courage to face the future.

Finally, we pray for those who have lost their fathers,
whether as children or as adults,
for some their father little more than a name,
for others, a heart-wrenching memory,
but each carrying a sense of loss.
Grant your strength, your comfort and your hope.

Father God,
we lift before you today fathers and their children.
Enfold them in your love,
and surround them with your fatherly care,
today and every day.
Through your Son, Jesus Christ our Lord.   *Nick Fawcett*

51 Father, give us all fatherly care.
Help fathers to reflect you
in the way they discharge their responsibilities.
May they be priests to their spouses
and to their children.   *Ray Simpson*

52 Gracious God,
you are the Creator of the ends of the earth,
and yet you call us your children.
You are greater than we can ever begin to imagine,
and yet you invite us to call you 'Our Father'.
Always you have loved us:
forgive our feeble response.

You do not keep us at arm's length,
remote in your holiness,
but you reach out your hands in love,
wanting us to relate to you, one to one.
Always you have loved us:
forgive our feeble response.

Gracious God,
forgive us that we call you 'Our Father',
but fail to live as your children.
We do not trust you as we should,
preferring instead to follow our own inclinations.
We are reluctant to accept your will,
repeatedly disobeying your instructions.
We are slow to seek your guidance,
but swift to forget you and wander from your side.
We all too rarely thank you for what we have,
but all too often complain
when we do not receive what we ask for.
Always you have loved us:
forgive our feeble response.

Gracious God,
we have returned your love by acting like spoilt children,
yet still you have kept faith.
Accept our thanks that, despite our wilfulness,
you refuse to give up on us,
working instead to draw us closer.
You are always there for us,
waiting to welcome us back
and set us on our feet again.
Always you have loved us:
forgive our feeble response.

Gracious God, our Father,
we praise and thank you for your undeserved goodness,
and we resolve today
to live more faithfully as your children.
Always you have loved us:
forgive our feeble response.
In the name of Jesus Christ, your Son, our Lord.

Nick Fawcett

Parents

Blessing of a new parent

53 May the delight you feel today
continue to fill and thrill you in the years ahead,
the privilege of nurturing a young life –
supporting and guiding,
protecting and providing –
offering a constant source of joy.
In the demands and duties of daily life,
may there always be time to listen,
share,
encourage
and enjoy –
time to appreciate the unique and priceless treasure
of parenthood.
God's blessing be upon you and your little one,
this and every day,
through Jesus Christ our Lord.   *Nick Fawcett*

54 There is nothing you can do
that would stop God loving you.
You are always his precious child.   *Susan Sayers*

55 Dear God,
I'm glad you love me.
I like being one of your children!   *Susan Sayers*

56 We pray for all parents with young children,
thanking you for them
and asking you to bless and guide their parenting;
we pray for families in debt;
for those whose homes have been repossessed,
and those whose financial security
makes them forgetful of your love.   *Susan Sayers*

57 Father of love,
accept the thanksgiving of these parents.
May their spirits, lifted to you now in humble gratitude,
always turn to you for help and strength.
Give them wisdom, tenderness and patience
to guide their child to know right from wrong. *Ray Simpson*

58 Father, may [name] and [name] be to each other
a strength in need, a comfort in sorrow,
a companion in joy.
Knit their wills together in your will,
that they may live together
in love, hope and peace
all of their days.   *Ray Simpson*

59 May the Three of Limitless Love
replenish our stock of love.
May those we care for not take us for granted. *Ray Simpson*

60 God give us grace to
listen to our loved ones,
play with our loved ones,
weep with our loved ones,
confront our loved ones,
explain things to our loved ones
and then to give them away
as a blessing to the world.   *Ray Simpson*

61 God help us to
listen to our loved ones,
play with our loved ones,
laugh with our loved ones,
weep with our loved ones,
forgive our loved ones,
take responsibility for our loved ones,
be faithful to our loved ones forever.   *Ray Simpson*

62 May God bless our own houses,
that they may be places of peace and hospitality.
May all those who visit us
sense something precious
that we have in loving God,
and in being loved by God.   *Gerald O'Mahony*

63 Mary and Joseph must have been bewildered
regarding God's wishes for their child.
We pray for all parents,
doing their best. *Gerald O'Mahony*

64 Simeon could see
that Jesus would be great,
but that Mary's heart would be broken
along the way.
We pray for all parents,
in their joys and in their heartbreaks. *Gerald O'Mahony*

65 The best guarantee of a happy maturity
is to start with a united family,
each respecting and loving the other(s).
We pray that the values of lifelong love
may be treasured and fostered. *Gerald O'Mahony*

Children

66 Living God,
Father of all,
we come today thanking you for the gift of this child,
with all the joy yet demands,
expectations yet responsibilities,
surrounding him/her.
We come also thanking you for the gift of eternal life,
new birth in Christ,
recognising equally the blessing yet challenge,
reward yet cost,
that this involves too.
Receive today the commitment that will be expressed
and vows made,
and, by your grace, lead each of us to discover in life now
the joy of life in all its fullness –
your gracious gift through Jesus Christ our Lord.
Nick Fawcett

67   Loving God,
we thank you for the gift of life and for the miracle of birth,
the wonder of a newborn child,
fashioned by your hand,
lovingly created,
and bringing such joy to so many.

We thank you for the life of AB,
for all that stretches before him/her –
the possibilities, joys and discoveries you hold in store,
the enrichment he/she will bring through his/her presence,
and the times we will share with him/her
over the years to come.

We thank you for the love that surrounds A –
the care of his/her parents,
the support of family and friends,
the prayers of this fellowship,
and your own everlasting arms.

We thank you for the happiness we share this day –
the joy A's birth has brought,
the hope it has kindled,
and the thanksgiving it has evoked.

We thank you for your gift of eternal life –
a life which begins here and now,
bringing peace, love and fulfilment,
yet which promises greater joys to come.

Loving God,
this is a day of thanksgiving, celebration and dedication,
a day to honour you
and to acknowledge your goodness.
Gladly we consecrate A to you
and joyfully we commit ourselves in the same faith.
Through Jesus Christ our Lord.   *Nick Fawcett*

68   The Lord watch over you, this and every day,
the Lord guide your footsteps and keep you from evil,
the Lord grant you health and strength, joy and fulfilment,
your whole life long.

The Lord be a blessing to you,
leading you in the way of peace, wisdom, love and humility,
so that you in turn may be a blessing to others.
The Lord fill you with light
and enfold you in love,
now and for evermore.
Through Jesus Christ our Lord   *Nick Fawcett.*

69 Creator God,
we worship you today for the gift of a new life.
We come with joy in our hearts,
to thank you for this child,
to praise you for all his/her birth means to us,
and all it means to you.
We thank you for the love that has brought A into being,
the care that surrounds him/her,
the excitement his/her arrival has brought,
and the happiness that he/she has given
to those around him/her.

Grant your blessing upon A.
Watch over him/her.
Guide his/her footsteps.
Protect him/her from danger.
Bless him/her with health.
Fill him/her with joy.
And in the fullness of your time
may he/she come to know your love,
and respond to you in faith,
discovering the joy and peace
that you alone can offer.

Creator God,
we pray also for C and D,
whom you have entrusted
with the responsibilities of parenthood –
give them wisdom,
patience,
devotion,
and dedication.

May A enrich their lives in immeasurable ways,
and may they in turn offer A the security
of a loving, caring home in which to grow.
Help them, through their words and actions,
to sow the seeds of your love in A's heart,
and then to give him/her space
to make his/her response in his/her own time and own way.

Creator God,
we thank you for this day,
this child,
and this family.
And we thank you for your love which surrounds us all,
this day and always.
Lord of life,
hear our prayer,
in the name of Christ.

Nick Fawcett

70   Gracious God,
we pray for AB in whatever the future may hold for him/her.
May your hand be there to lead,
and your love be there to bless.

Grant help to A in times of learning,
so that he/she may grow in wisdom and understanding,
in knowledge, skill and ability,
and in experience and character,
equipped to make the most of life's possibilities.
May your hand be there to lead,
and your love be there to bless.

Grant A your strength in times of testing –
the ability to overcome difficulties,
withstand trials,
and conquer temptation,
staying true to his/her convictions
and emerging stronger out of adversity.
May your hand be there to lead,
and your love be there to bless.

Grant your guidance in times of uncertainty –
discernment as to the right way forward,
patience in coming to a decision,
and confidence that a door will open,
your will ultimately becoming apparent.
May your hand be there to lead,
and your love be there to bless.

Grant your peace in times of turmoil –
the knowledge that, whatever may happen, you are there,
nothing ever able to separate us from your love,
and so may A be able
to meet changing circumstances of life with equanimity,
assured of your ultimate purpose.
May your hand be there to lead,
and your love be there to bless.

Grant your blessing in times of opportunity,
so that A may discover lasting love,
enduring joy,
and fulfilment in work, faith and life.
May your hand be there to lead,
and your love be there to bless.

Gracious God,
we ask you to put your hand upon A,
to watch over him/her,
to direct his/her footsteps
and to make known your love,
so that he/she may respond freely to you
in his/her own time and way.
May your hand be there to lead,
and your love be there to bless.
In the name of Christ we ask it.   *Nick Fawcett*

71   Gracious God,
      we thank you for your gift of children,
      for the joy, the laughter,
      and the fun they bring in so many ways.
      We thank you for their innate zest for life –
      the interest, excitement and fascination they find
      in so much we count ordinary.

We thank you for their special qualities –
their innocence, trust, enthusiasm, energy,
and sheer hunger to learn.
We lift them now to you:
open your heart to all.

We pray for this child presented to you this day,
and for children everywhere,
so precious to us,
so precious to you.
Watch over them,
protect them, guide them and bless them.
And hear also our prayer for those who are childless,
or who long to conceive another child.
Reach out to them in their pain, their frustration,
their disappointment, their anger.
Help them not to lose hope until all hope is past,
and if that time finally comes
give them the comfort you alone can bring,
and courage to channel their love to those around them.

Finally we pray for disadvantaged children –
those who are disabled, abused, orphaned,
undernourished, unloved, unwanted –
so many denied the start in life they deserve
and the care they need.
Loving God,
in Christ you welcomed little children,
demonstrating their importance to you,
their special place in your heart.
Prosper the work of all who care for children today –
all who strive to give them a better life,
a brighter future,
a safer world in which to grow.
Use them, and us, to make real your care for all.

Nick Fawcett

72 Jesus, friend of little children,
    your message belongs to them first of all,
    not to the wise and learned.

Look after our children in your love,
keep them safe,
and may we learn your wisdom from them.

Gerald O'Mahony

73   May we, and our children,
    learn to love and appreciate
    the one and only life we have,
    and to make the most of it.   *Gerald O'Mahony*

74   The young Jesus grew in wisdom,
    and our own children
    can sometimes astonish us by their wisdom.
    May we ourselves learn
    from their unspoiled eyes.   *Gerald O'Mahony*

75   Children are always full of surprises,
    in some ways just like their parents,
    in other ways quite different.
    We pray that all parents
    may allow their children
    to be their new selves.   *Gerald O'Mahony*

76   We see from the gospels how Jesus loves little children,
    and thinks very highly of each one of them.
    May he bless the children in our parish,
    and bless their parents.
    May all who teach them know and understand
    that great reverence is owed to little children.

Gerald O'Mahony

77   Gracious God,
    you have brought this child into being –
    go with him/her now in their journey of life.
    May he/she know joy,
    health,
    and peace.
    May he/she grow in love,
    wisdom,
    and faith.

Direct his/her steps,
keep him/her from evil,
and help him/her to live life in all its fullness,
this day and always.
In the name of Christ   *Nick Fawcett*

Blessing of a newborn child

78 God be praised for the joy you have brought
and the delight that surrounds you.
God provide for and protect you,
granting you health,
wisdom,
peace
and joy.
God guide your footsteps,
and equip you for your journey, wherever it might lead.
God be with those who love you,
and those you will love in turn,
that you and they will taste his goodness
and celebrate the life he offers in all its fullness,
through Jesus Christ our Lord.   *Nick Fawcett*

Blessing of a premature child

79 Lord Jesus Christ,
born as a baby into a hostile and dangerous world,
watch over this little one,
so vulnerable yet so precious,
so tiny yet carrying such hopes
and inspiring such enormous love.
Cherish, protect, support and strengthen,
so that [Name] may grow in health and strength,
wisdom and maturity,
experiencing joy
and bringing it to others.
In your name we pray.   *Nick Fawcett*

Blessing of a mentally disabled child

80 [Name],
may God watch over you,
granting you the care, support,
love and provision you need.
May he give wisdom, dedication,
help and strength to your parents
and to all who will look after you,
and through the loving, patient nurture
that surrounds you,
may you find inner pleasure,
peace,
security
and true contentment.   *Nick Fawcett*

Blessing of a physically disabled child

81 Almighty God,
though disability will bring difficulty,
give [Name] strength to overcome it,
helping her/him to find joy, blessing and fulfilment
in all life holds.
Grant her/him patience,
courage,
resilience
and determination,
and, above all, the knowledge that s/he
is a unique person,
precious in her/his own right,
a whole person with as much to contribute
as anyone.
In that assurance may s/he live each moment.   *Nick Fawcett*

Blessing of a child with learning difficulties

82 Loving God,
watch over [Name]
and grant her/him the care,
encouragement
and provision s/he needs to realise her/his potential.

Through the devotion of parent/s and family,
the support of friends
and the dedication of teachers,
instil self-belief,
enthusiasm,
resilience
and resourcefulness,
equipping her/him to meet the challenges ahead,
through Jesus Christ our Lord. *Nick Fawcett*

Blessing of a child starting school

83 May God bless you, [Name],
in the time you will spend at school,
and equip you through it
with the resources you need for the journey of life.
May you find pleasure in learning,
enrichment through friendships
and fun through shared activities,
your education helping you to grow
not only in knowledge but also as a person.
God protect you from harm,
equip you with wisdom
and enfold you in love,
granting you joy now
and fulfilment in the years to come,
through Jesus Christ our Lord. *Nick Fawcett*

Blessing of a young person before an examination

84 At this stressful time, Lord,
grant your peace –
composure of mind
and serenity of spirit –
that the long hours of work, study and revision
leading up to this exam
may bear fruit,
receiving their due reward.
Help [Name] simply to give of his/her best,
and, having done that, to rest content,
knowing that no one could ask for more.
In your name we ask it. *Nick Fawcett*

Blessing of a son or daughter leaving home

85 God bless you, [Name], for the joy you've brought,
the help you've given
and love you've shared –
everything you've contributed to this home and family
in so many ways
across so many years.
As you travel now from the old to the new,
wherever you might be and whatever life might bring,
may God go with you –
a light to your path
and a companion along your way –
his hand there to guide and his arms to embrace,
bringing the knowledge
that you are as close to his heart
as you will always be to ours.   *Nick Fawcett*

Blessing of parents/a parent when a daughter or son leaves home

86 May God be with you at this time of change,
in the contrasting emotions you feel –
the pride . . .
and the pain,
the love . . .
and the loss,
the sense of responsibility fulfilled . . .
but also of a chapter closing.
May he help you to let go . . .
yet also stay close,
to keep in contact . . .
yet also leave space;
to be there when needed . . .
yet also to let [Name] make her/his own decisions,
finding joy in her/his freedom . . .
but equally in your own,
discovering new avenues for your love,
new uses for your time,
and new directions in your life,
God walking with you and all you hold dear,
this and every day.   *Nick Fawcett*

Blessing of a university/college fresher

87 Grant to [Name], Lord, at this exciting yet daunting time,
this time of embracing the new
and moving on from the old,
a sure and certain knowledge of your presence,
your guidance,
and your love that come what may, will not fail.
Grant the ability to work but also to rest,
to study but also to socialise,
to embrace new insights but also to keep hold of truth,
to welcome all that is good in student life
but also to resist whatever is bad,
knowing when to say yes, and when no.
Watch over [Name],
equip and enable him/her
for all the challenges and opportunities that lie ahead,
and so may he/she find true fulfilment,
now and in the years ahead. *Nick Fawcett*

88 We thank you, loving God,
for giving us one another to enjoy,
to laugh and cry with, to learn to live with.
May even our conflicts and arguments be used
in helping us to grow up in your love. *Susan Sayers*

89 All the other people in the world
are your sisters and brothers
because God made
and loves all of us. *Susan Sayers*

Infant blessing
Three drops of warm water are poured on the baby's forehead,
one during each of the first three sentences
90 A little drop of your Creator
on your forehead, precious one. Amen.
A little drop of your Saviour
on your forehead, precious one. Amen.
A little drop of your Guardian Spirit
on your forehead, precious one. Amen.

The little drop of the Three
to shield you from harm
to fill you with their virtue. Amen.   *Ray Simpson*

91 God our Creator,
in giving us this child you have shown us your love.
We thank you from our hearts for the joy of this child,
for the wonder of this life,
for a safe delivery
and for the privilege of being parents.   *Ray Simpson*

Children's rooms

92 May the loving Father God
always be here with you
and make you feel safe.
May friendly Jesus
always be here with you
and make you feel happy.
May his kindly Spirit
always be here with you
to listen to you.
May you enjoy their company as you play.
May angels look after you when you sleep
and when you dream,
and help you to wake with a smile on your face.
                                                       Ray Simpson

School

93 Lord, circle this school and keep these good things within:
eagerness to learn,
flowering of talents,
a sense of wonder,
enjoyment of sport,
experience of beauty,
warmth of friendship,
appreciation of arts,
respect for all,
service of others,
teamwork between children and adults,

care for the planet,
reverence for life,
fitness of body, mind and spirit.
Lord, circle this school and keep these bad things without:
low self-esteem,
confusion,
prejudice,
pride,
bullying,
cheating,
stealing,
fear of appraisal,
malicious gossip,
absenteeism,
'couldn't care less' attitudes.
Lord, circle this school,
for you are the source of all that is good and true.

Ray Simpson

For a person joining a school

94 May smiling faces welcome you.
May helping hands welcome you.
May kind teachers welcome you.
May fears fly away,
temper go away,
fibs stay away.
May you make new friends,
learn new things,
grow strong limbs.
May God make you thoughtful,
Jesus make you happy,
Spirit make you friendly.   *Ray Simpson*

Leaving school

95 Dear God,
we've come to the end of our school years
with mixed feelings.
As we look back and as we look to what is coming,
we see all sorts of shapes and colours in flow and flux.

God of shapes and colours, bless these to us
and be in the flow and flux.
As we look back and as we look to what is coming,
we see all sorts of empty gaps.
God of the gaps, fill these for us
and be in the flow and flux.
As we look back, bless us with forgiveness
and the knowledge that nothing need be wasted with you.
As we look forward, help us find what work is right for us.
Bless our questioning and finding out.
Will we get jobs?
Bless our work and all the talents you have put within us;
may they grow wherever we shall be.
Be a vision to guide us, a voice to lead us,
a Saviour to forgive us, a hand to hold us,
a friend to teach us for ever.   *Ray Simpson*

A baby

96 May this little one
bring love and affection to you
and good to the world.
May this be a day of grace for you.
May you be a guarding one to this gift of heaven,
along with the saints and the angels
and the Three of Limitless Love.   *Ray Simpson*

A boy's first steps towards manhood

97 God help you to
run straight,
speak what is true,
ask questions,
overcome fear,
learn self-control;
bear failure,
stand alone,
care for your body,
guard your soul;
honour women,
respect men,

explore the world,
give your best;
open your heart to all people,
close your heart to all pretence,
know yourself;
reverence the Creator,
walk with the Saviour,
flow with the Spirit,
enter into your eternal destiny.   *Ray Simpson*

A girl's first period

98 This is a blessing of the God of life,
the blessing of mild mother Mary,
from whose breasts our Lord suckled milk.
May the Spirit bathe you and make you to grow wise.
May God give you strength in every such time.
May Christ give you love in every such time.
May Spirit give you peace in every such time.
Lord, place these nine choice graces in the upturned face
of this day's wakened lass:
the grace of deportment,
the grace of voice,
the grace of provision,
the grace of goodness,
the grace of wisdom,
the grace of caring,
the grace of femininity,
the grace of a lovely personality,
the grace of godly speech.   *Ray Simpson*

Baby

99 You are made in the likeness
of the good Birther, little one.
May good grow in you.
You are made in the likeness
of the Compassionate Saviour, little one.
May compassion grow in you.
You are made in the likeness
of the creative Spirit, little one.

May creativity grow in you.
You are made in the likeness
of the Three's Eternal Dance, little one.
May fun and laughter grow in you.   *Ray Simpson*

Stepchildren

100 The family of God draw round you,
the family of God to welcome you,
the family of God to listen to you,
the family of God to cherish you,
the family of God to heal you.
Mary, the mother of our Lord,
Joseph at his work,
the saints of heaven,
your guardian angels
and we, your new loved ones.
May heaven's gate of welcome open wide;
may our heart of welcome open wide;
may your heart of welcome open wide,
this day and always.   *Ray Simpson*

101 A family of friends to draw round you.
A family to cherish you and introduce you to new things.
The family of God to draw round you –
Mary, the mother of Jesus,
Joseph in his workplace –
opening heaven's gates to welcome you.   *Ray Simpson*

Toddler

102 The three palmfuls of the Sacred Three
to preserve you from every envy or evil eye:
the palmful of the Father of life,
the palmful of the Christ of love,
the palmful of the Spirit of peace,
the God of threefold love.   *Ray Simpson*

103 Wisdom of years be yours.
Joy of friendships be yours.
Wealth of memories be yours.

Fruit of endeavour be yours.
Hope of heaven be yours.
Peace of God's child be yours.

Ray Simpson

104 God of first and last,
protect the unborn,
conceived in love,
deserving of your grace and favour.
Bring them to full life
as a testimony to your faithfulness,
as a test of our responsibility.
As we remember your Son's name,
may we never forget the role of Mary,
our Saviour's safeguard,
from conception to birth,
to death and resurrection.

Rupert Bristow

105 Lord unseen, but known,
have mercy on offspring known but not yet seen,
whether conceived in love or lust.
May they have equal rights to your love;
may they have equal love from those around them;
so that they may grow in confidence,
grow in faith, grow in showing the love to others
that they were shown by your grace,
and by our fond care.

Rupert Bristow

106 God of grace,
you see into our hearts and minds.
You also see before and after in time and space.
We thank you for all the love shown to us
before we came into this world.
And just as you care for us now,
in preparation for the world to come,
so may we give special thought and prayer
for the yet unborn;
for the stillborn;
for those who struggle even before birth;
and for those who struggle in infancy.

Rupert Bristow

107   Heavenly Father,
you know the pangs of creation
and importance of rest.
Help mothers and fathers to show
the same love of their creation
that you have shown to us.
May the joys ahead herald a new relationship,
in the same way as the bright star over Bethlehem
heralded a new birth, a new beginning,
in your relationship with humankind.   *Rupert Bristow*

Children's Prayers

108   Jesus, you helped your dad in a woodwork shop.
You made nice things out of wood.
We are like wood in your hands.
Sometimes we are hard.
Please make us into nice people.   *Ray Simpson*

109   Dear Jesus,
some people don't notice us and we feel left out.
You were not like that –
you noticed people and put yourself in their shoes.
Help us to notice people and put ourselves in their shoes.
Help us to feel for them and be friends   *Ray Simpson*

110   Good morning, God.
How are you?
I am OK, but sometimes I get upset.
Help me to do things your way.   *Ray Simpson*

111   Dear God, when we wake up,
may we feel the sun is shining on us
because you are smiling down on us.
Chase away bad, dark thoughts.
Make us smile.   *Ray Simpson*

Midday

112 Stop!
It's the middle of the day.
We get too full of ourselves.
Please, God,
calm us down.   *Ray Simpson*

Evening

113 Mr Sun, you settle down.
God made you, God made us.
Mr God,
help us to think before we speak
and settle down with you.   *Ray Simpson*

114 Dear God,
if you came to church
we would feel happy.
We might
clap
or laugh
or cry
or dance
or paint
or sing
or show you our playthings
or just sit quietly.
Help us make church like that anyway,
ready for you to turn up any time.   *Ray Simpson*

115 Teach us, dear God, to
know you better,
explore your world,
learn from mistakes,
understand others,
use our talents,
remember important things,
and grow like Jesus.   *Ray Simpson*

116 Dear Jesus,
there is a good voice
and a bad voice inside us.
Help us to listen to the good voice
and throw out the bad voice.   *Ray Simpson*

117 Teach us to dance like clouds that play.
Teach us to laugh like sun that glistens.
Teach us to flow like streams that sing.
Teach us to fly like birds that chirp.
Teach us to dream like rainbows that gleam.
Teach us to have fun with you.   *Ray Simpson*

118 Jesus,
bless our eyes – so we notice others.
Bless our hearts – so we love others.
Bless our hands – so we help others.
Where there is hate, let us bring love.
Where there are quarrels, let us bring peace.
Where there is darkness, let us bring light.
Where there is sadness, let us bring joy.   *Ray Simpson*

119 God bless the air.
Help us not to spoil it.
God bless the sea.
Help us not to poison it.
God bless the earth.
Help us not to trample it.
God bless the planet.
Help us not to ruin it.
God bless here.
Help us look after it.   *Ray Simpson*

120 When we eat our food,
may we think of the earth that gives it.
When we have rides in a car,
may we think of the oil that moves it.
When we buy something in a shop,
may we think of the people who made it.
When we go to sleep,
may we think of you who creates us.   *Ray Simpson*

121 Dear Jesus,
the Church is your world family.
You have given treasures
to different parts of this family
and we don't know what they are.
Help us, in our church,
to find different treasures like
the Bible,
the Holy Spirit,
friends,
stillness,
communion,
beautiful art,
the saints,
the poor,
celebrations,
prayer,
and other things
we have not yet thought of.   *Ray Simpson*

122 Our Father in heaven,
your kingdom come, your will be done
on Earth as it is in heaven.
Your kingdom come
because we are honest and do not cheat;
because we are fair and do not steal;
because we listen and do not laugh at others;
because we are friends and do not gossip;
because we love and do not hate;
because we share and do not grab.   *Ray Simpson*

123 Dear God,
help us make a church without walls;
help us to pray all over the place;
help us to have parties wherever there's space;
help us to visit, play and tell stories
to new and old friends.
Dear God, who is present to all,
put your love in our hearts and draw others to you.
                                                    Ray Simpson

124   Father, thank you for bringing me through the night,
and thank you for a new day.
Help me to come closer to you today.
If I forget you,
please don't you forget me.   *Gerald O'Mahony*

125   When we get so afraid over some secret trouble,
that we don't dare to share the secret with someone who
could help,
give us courage, dear Jesus,
and give us the wisdom to know who to share with.
      Gerald O'Mahony

126   When we don't do the right thing
because other children might laugh at us,
then please make us brave
to do the thing that pleases you, friend Jesus,
the best friend we will ever have.   *Gerald O'Mahony*

127   God our Father,
remind us always to say thank you
to the people who help us.
That will make them feel like
helping us again.   *Gerald O'Mahony*

128   For the times we could have helped people,
especially old or sick people,
and we just couldn't be bothered:
God our Father, we are sorry.   *Gerald O'Mahony*

129   Thank you, God, for all the things we can do easily,
that older people find difficult.
We can touch our toes (legs straight)
and they mostly cannot . . .
And a thousand other things
we can do that they can't do.
Make us grateful, and willing to share our gifts.
      Gerald O'Mahony

Homes and Families

Blessing of the elderly

130 Eternal God,
reach out in love,
and support those for whom advancing years
bring trials.
Though health may fade and faculties fail,
strength decline and vigour wane,
grant the assurance that your grace is the same
yesterday, today and tomorrow,
a fixed point in a world of change.
So, then, in your mercy,
grant help and strength,
comfort and joy,
and, above all, confidence in your enduring purpose –
the knowledge that,
come what may,
your love will never let us go.   *Nick Fawcett*

131 Loving God,
bless and guide us and our families
through all the troubles and chances of life,
supporting one another in love
and forgiving one another every day.   *Susan Sayers*

132 Bless our homes and families
and all our neighbours and friends;
train us to listen to one another with full attention,
and recognise one another's gifts.   *Susan Sayers*

133 Lord, you know the need and pain
of those we love and worry about.
As you look after them,
give them the sense of your caring presence
to uphold and sustain them.   *Susan Sayers*

134 God bless my family.
Look after us all.
Help us look after each other.
In life and death
keep us safe for ever.   *Susan Sayers*

135 Father, we thank you
     for the personal and affectionate way you care for us
     and provide for all our needs;
     may we spread the good news of your love
     by the way we respond to you and to one another.
                                              Susan Sayers

136 Father, in love we stand alongside
     all whose lives are bound up with ours.
     Work with tenderness in the relationships
     we bring before you now.   *Susan Sayers*

137 Father, we offer our homes and our relationships
     for you to work in and transform;
     we offer you our meetings and conflicts
     and all differences of opinion
     for you to use to your glory.   *Susan Sayers*

138 Father, may our homes, schools and churches
     reflect and engender the Godly values
     of mutual care, respect and responsibility, *Susan Sayers*
     of integrity and forgiveness.

139 Within our homes and places of work
     may we practise self-discipline in all that we say,
     and in the way it is said,
     using our mouths to speak wisely and positively
     with love in both hearts and voices. *Susan Sayers*

140 Lord, we welcome you into our homes,
     our streets, and our communities;
     where we are blind to your presence,
     give us sight;
     in the ordinary and the remarkable,
     help us to recognise our true and living God. *Susan Sayers*

141 Father, work your love in our homes,
     making them places of welcome,
     understanding and forgiveness.   *Susan Sayers*

142   Father, we ask for your faithful presence
in our homes, and all the homes in this parish;
pour out your spirit of patience and forgiveness
wherever the sparks fly.
Susan Sayers

143   Walk with us, Lord, down the streets
of our cities, towns and villages,
drive with us down the motorways
and fly with us down the air corridors.
Meet all those who are curious, searching,
or moving in the wrong direction.
Let your presence be sought
and recognised in all the world.
Susan Sayers

144   Wherever there is illness, unhappiness,
injustice or fear;
wherever people feel frustrated,
imprisoned or trapped;
give us a greater sense of loving community,
a heart to put right whatever we can,
and the willingness to stand
alongside one another in our sorrows.
Susan Sayers

145   Lord, in the local issues of this community,
and in the difficulties and dilemmas
on the world stage,
may we look for the face of Christ
and fix our attention on his underlying values
of love, justice and mercy.
Susan Sayers

146   We pray for those who are called to look after
loved ones
and build up the local community,
that they may be filled with your love and kindness.
Susan Sayers

147   May the way we live help other people
to get to know you better.
Susan Sayers

148 We pray for our families and our friends,
that we may treat one another with love and respect.
Susan Sayers

149 We pray that within our homes and communities
there may be a new awareness
of one another's gifts and needs,
more sensitivity and respect in our relationships;
may we reverence one another as fellow beings,
born of your creative love.
Susan Sayers

150 Wherever our homes are lacking
in love and mutual respect,
wherever destructive relationships
cause distress and heartache,
and wherever people are made to feel they don't matter,
give a new realisation of your ways
and your hopes for us, so that your kingdom may come
and your will be done.
Susan Sayers

151 Lord, in all the minor squabbles
and major rifts of family life,
may we know the assurance of your promise
to be with us always,
and your power to transform and renew.
Susan Sayers

152 Father, we want to take more seriously
our community commitment to our children.
Show us what needs to be started,
developed or changed in our attitudes to one another,
and in the way we help one another's faith to grow.
Susan Sayers

153 God of loving kindness,
watch over our homes and families,
our friends and neighbours;
we pray too for those who wish us harm
and those we find it difficult to love;
we pray for more of you in all our relationships.
Susan Sayers

154 Father, we thank you for the joy
of our families and friendships,
and the opportunities provided in our homes
for learning what real loving is all about.
We pray for those we love and worry about,
and those who love and worry about us,
commending one another to your keeping.   *Susan Sayers*

155 Lord of all, wherever families are struggling
to stay together,
and wherever there are ongoing arguments
and family feuds,
we ask your anointing for tranquillity and harmony.
Wherever children are unwanted and unloved,
neglected or in danger, we ask your protection and help.
                                        Susan Sayers

156 Heavenly Father, make our homes
places of love and growth,
welcoming to all who visit them,
and accepting and forgiving to all who are nurtured there.
Help us through the quarrels and heartaches
and remind us to honour one another
as your cherished ones.   *Susan Sayers*

157 Fill our homes and neighbourhoods, O Lord,
with the generosity and trust that allows space
but is always ready to encourage and support.
May we cherish our bodies, minds and spirits
as temples containing your Spirit,
and honour one another as people of your making.
                                        Susan Sayers

158 Merciful God, break all habits
of destructive behaviour
in our homes and families, our friendships
and in all the homes of this parish.
Develop our ability to celebrate what is good
and face what is not with honesty.   *Susan Sayers*

159   Loving Father,
      may our closeness to family and friends
      make us never exclusive, shutting others out,
      but always inclusive, welcoming others in.
      Encourage us in outgoing hospitality
      and keep us from becoming
      possessive with those we love.   *Susan Sayers*

160   Loving God, we thank you
      for the nurturing we have received,
      and pray for our children and young people as they grow.
      Protect them from evil and strengthen them in faith;
      may they continue to be yours for ever.   *Susan Sayers*

161   Loving God, may the ways we manage our homes,
      decisions, time and money be in keeping with our calling
      as inheritors of the kingdom.
      May your love undergird all our loving.   *Susan Sayers*

162   Wherever ongoing family conflicts need resolving,
      wherever communication has broken down,
      develop our capacity for unconditional loving,
      and appreciation of every 'other'
      as another child of your creating.   *Susan Sayers*

163   God of accepting love,
      drive far from our homes and communities
      all rejection and devaluing;
      all justification for barriers;
      and give us the courage to reach out in love.   *Susan Sayers*

164   With the statistics of family life
      challenging our values,
      and with the pressures to conform to norms
      in conflict with God's will,
      we pray for your sound and centred wisdom
      in all our daily living and life choices.   *Susan Sayers*

165 Heavenly Father, we pray for breadwinners
and sandwich makers, and all food growers;
for your presence in kitchens, dining rooms,
canteens, restaurants and bars;
wherever people gather to eat together,
may they find you there with them.   *Susan Sayers*

166 We pray for our loved ones;
for those who lift our hearts
and those who turn our hair grey.
We pray for those we instinctively warm to
and those with whom
there are frequent misunderstandings.
We thank God for our opportunities of forgiveness.
                                              Susan Sayers

167 We thank you for all our blessings
and pray that we may take none of them
for granted,
but commit ourselves to live out
our thanks each day.   *Susan Sayers*

168 Father, come into our homes
and make them places of welcome
where your love is woven into all our relationships.
                                              Susan Sayers

169 We pray that we may take seriously
our responsibilities for nurturing our children
and those who do not yet know God's love.
Transform our living to reveal that love.   *Susan Sayers*

170 God of tenderness,
dwell in our homes
through all the times of joy
and all the heartaches and sadness,
teaching us to show one another
the love you show to us.   *Susan Sayers*

171 Whenever tempers are frayed
and patience is wearing thin,
give us space to collect ourselves and try again.
Whenever the demands of family and friends
remind us of our limitations,
minister graciously through our weakness
and teach us the humility of apologising.   *Susan Sayers*

172 May our care of the very young and the elderly
imitate the faithful and generous caring of our God;
may we overcome our envies, jealousies and grievances,
so that in God's love we can look at one another face to face,
and practise the liberating work of forgiveness. *Susan Sayers*

173 As we call to mind our loved ones,
all who depend on us,
and those on whom we depend,
all with whom we laugh, cry, work or play,
cleanse and refresh our relationships
and give us greater love, understanding and forgiveness.
                                                  Susan Sayers

174 Thank you, Lord God, for our families and friends,
those we meet each day and those we seldom see;
draw all our loved ones closer to you,
and search out those whose faith
is fragile or fragmented.   *Susan Sayers*

175 We long for our homes to be filled with God's love,
so we are happy to put ourselves out for others,
to listen with full attention, and to value one another.
We long to clear away anything in our lifestyle
which competes with God for our commitment.
                                                  Susan Sayers

176 May all the families on earth
be blessed with mutual love
and caring consideration one of another;

may arguments and misunderstandings
be properly resolved,
and difficult relationships refreshed and healed. *Susan Sayers*

177 We pray for all our relatives
and the family life of our country,
longing for the grace to love and honour
one another,
to trust and to persevere.   *Susan Sayers*

178 We pray for the very young and the very old,
for mothers, fathers and children
and all the homes in this parish.   *Susan Sayers*

A prayer for family, godparents and friends
179 May you respect one another;
may the goodness of friendship grow in you;
may the love that covers a multitude of sins be upon you.
God's peace be with you, whatever you do;
God's light to guide you wherever you go;
God's goodness to fill you and help you to grow.
                                                       Ray Simpson

For the household
180 We place into your hands
all people who will live together here.
May they know that everything here is yours,
and they belong here.
May they sense your love here.
May the presence of the Three Kindly Persons
free each to accept personal pain,
to grow through each stage of development,
to give space to others,
to express feelings,
to forgive from the heart,
to flower as a person.   *Ray Simpson*

On returning home

181 May our homes reflect your presence,
coming through the personalities you have given us.
Grace us to express
your peace and perfect order into them.
Remind us to acknowledge your authority
over all that will be thought, purchased and arranged.
Give us a fresh supply of truth and beauty
on which to draw as we relax, entertain, work and sleep.
Ray Simpson

182 God bless our families.
May we be there for one another.
May we respect each one's unique personality.
May we learn to take things in our stride.
May we pray, have fun and forgive.   *Ray Simpson*

183 May the Three Loves in God's heart
free us to
enjoy each other's company,
accept each other's pain,
express our needs,
forgive from our hearts,
that we may flower as people.   *Ray Simpson*

184 God protect the household.
God consecrate the children.
God encompass our assets.   *Ray Simpson*

TV

185 God make the TV
a blessing to the family.
When there's horrible stuff,
may we turn the switch off.
When there's too much choice,
may we listen to your voice.
May the people in the soap
not give up hope.

When the top spots show off,
may we say 'that's enough'.
May the world out there
also get on air.
What in heaven is seen –
may it get on our screen.   *Ray Simpson*

When away from home

186 We release into your hands, O Lord,
our homes,
those for whom we love and care,
any who are dependent on us
who may feel vulnerable without us.
Lord, you love those whom we love.
We release into your hands, O Lord,
those for whom we have responsibilities,
those who are in need at this time,
those we have supported.
Lord, you care for all those for whom we care.
We release into your hands, O Lord,
our work,
the pressures that weary us,
the problems that would pursue us,
the things we have forgotten,
the tasks left unfinished.
Lord, you rule over all things.   *Ray Simpson*

187 We give thanks for the wonder of life,
for growth and for change.
We pray for our parents
and for those who have helped us to grow and learn.
We ask your blessing upon all who care for families
who are in trouble or in difficulty.   *David Adam*

188 We give you thanks for our homes and our loved ones.
In our busy lives
help us to make sure we have time
for each other and for you.   *David Adam*

189   We give thanks that your Holy Spirit
came upon the disciples in an ordinary home.
Bless our homes with your presence
and grant that there we may grow in the fruits of the Spirit.
Let us know you are with our loved ones and us.
Protect us from all evil
and guide us by your Spirit
in the ways of peace and love.   *David Adam*

190   Lord, in our homes help us to listen to each other
with undivided attention.
Teach us to be sensitive to the various calls for us
to share and to care for each other.
We ask you to protect our homes and loved ones.
                                                 David Adam

191   We give thanks for our homes and our loved ones,
for our godparents and our godchildren.
We ask your blessing upon them.
We remember all who come from broken homes
or who are suffering from broken relationships.
                                                 David Adam

192   We give thanks for our homes
and for all who love us.
May we show your presence in our daily living.
We pray for homes where there is neglect or lack of love,
where there is cruelty or deep selfishness.
We remember all who live alone
and those who are lonely.   *David Adam*

193   Bless our homes with the light of your presence.
We pray for our loved ones and friends,
for our neighbours and our community.
May the bright light of Christ shine within us
and scatter any darkness that is around us.   *David Adam*

194 We give thanks that Jesus was born into an earthly home
and shared in our daily life.
May we know that our homes and loved ones
are part of your kingdom.
We ask your blessing on homes
where there is strife and division, deceit and distrust.

David Adam

195 Lord, born into an ordinary home,
come to our homes,
that they may reflect your peace and your glory.
We ask your blessing upon all our loved ones,
those with whom we share this day
and those who are not able to be with us.   *David Adam*

196 As the Holy Family shared in an ordinary home,
we ask your blessing upon our homes.
May our homes reveal your presence
and our relationships increase our love for you.
We remember all homeless peoples,
all refugees and those who belong to homes
where there is violence or lack of love.   *David Adam*

197 We thank you, God, for the love of our homes.
Thank you for the love and care of our mothers.
We pray for families where a loved one is ill
or causing trouble.
We remember all who are suffering from lack of love,
and those who live in homes where there is tension
and broken relationships.   *David Adam*

198 Father of all,
we rejoice in the joys of family.
May we seek always to develop our roles,
as child, parent, carer or relative,
so that we encourage relationship,
model faithfulness,
empower development,
and acknowledge weaknesses.

Give us discernment and humility
as our roles change,
over time and in love.

Rupert Bristow

199   Enabler, Comforter,
give us insight, peace and love,
as we work out our relationships,
with you, with family, with friends.
May we give of ourselves
as we receive from others.
May we share our experience
where relevant and where needed.
May we keep our counsel
when we have nothing to add.
May we play our part,
in community, parish and network,
so that all benefit,
and no one is diminished.

Rupert Bristow

Families in Need

200   We pray for families suffering poverty
or financial difficulties,
for families full of tension and disagreement,
and for families coping with grief or separation.
We pray for the extended families represented here.
We pray for better awareness
of how our behaviour affects others.

Susan Sayers

201   We pray for the healing
of hurts and tensions in our families;
and for our friends,
thanking you for the blessings they give;
as friends of Christ, may we be
generous in our friendships.

Susan Sayers

Battered families
202   God of tender, loving care,
bless these, your battered children.
Take the pain out of their lives.

Take the fear out of their lives.
Take the despair out of their lives.
Take the resentment out of their lives,
and fill them with your gentle, healing love.   *Ray Simpson*

203   Gentle Father,
bless these battered children.
Take the hurt out of their lives.
May your gentle spirit flow
through all those who care for them.   *Ray Simpson*

204   Tender Saviour,
bless these battered wives.
Take the fear out of their lives.
May your tender spirit flow
through all those who care for them.   *Ray Simpson*

205   Caressing Spirit,
bless these elderly who feel battered
by their children's rejection.
Take resentment out of their lives.
May your caressing spirit flow
through all those who care for them.   *Ray Simpson*

206   The Divine Gift come into your loss.
The Divine Peace come into your dread.
The Divine Hope come into your despair.
The Divine Helper come to your aid.   *Ray Simpson*

207   Into your loss,
come,
O Being of Gift,
O Being of Peace,
O Being of Life eternal.
Into your threat,
come,
O Being of Strength,
O Being of Peace,
O Being of Life eternal.

Into your despair,
come,
O Being of Hope,
O Being of Peace,
O Being of Life eternal.
Into your devastation,
come,
O Being of Love,
O Being of Peace,
O Being of Life eternal.   *Ray Simpson*

208 Bruised?
The blessing of acceptance be yours.
Bitter?
The blessing of forgiveness be yours.
Angry?
The blessing of gentleness be yours.
Suicidal?
The blessing of trust be yours.
Broken?
The blessing of immortality be yours.   *Ray Simpson*

Tragedy
209 The blessing of acceptance be yours.
The blessing of forgiveness be yours.
The blessing of gentleness be yours.
The blessing of resilience be yours.
The blessing of eternal life be yours.   *Ray Simpson*

210 Come, Lord, let your presence be known
in our homes and in our lives.
Bless us in all our relationships
and dealings with others.
Come, Lord, with your light and love
to lives that are struggling with poverty and debt,
with bad housing and broken-down communities.
                                              David Adam

211   We thank you for our homes
and the love and acceptance that is there.
We pray for homes where life is oppressive
or adventure smothered.
We remember all who are leaving home for the first time
and all their loved ones.
We give you thanks for homes
where there are new members of the family
and where all are growing in love.   *David Adam*

212   We rejoice in the protection and the peace of our homes.
We thank you for our families and friends
and ask your blessing upon them.
We pray for families who have become bored with life
and with each other,
for couples who have lost the spirit of exploration
and adventure.   *David Adam*

213   We give thanks for the care and protection of our homes,
especially for all who have shared their lives
and their love with us.
We pray for all who come from homes
where there is discouragement
or a lack of love and understanding.
We remember especially
any children who have been taken into care.   *David Adam*

214   We ask that your love may be experienced in our homes
and among our loved ones and friends.
We pray for homes where there is conflict,
violence or abuse,
especially for any who live in fear
or feel unable to change.   *David Adam*

215   We ask your blessing on homes
that are suffering from great debt
or where the household is unable to cope
through various troubles.   *David Adam*

216 We ask your blessing upon our families and friends,
all whom we love and all who love us.
We remember homes where there is serious illness
and where loved ones are carers.
We pray especially for all who are struggling
to keep their homes together,
all whose physical or financial resources are running out.

David Adam

217 We remember homes where people are not coping well,
where there are struggles in relationships.
We remember especially homes
where there are great tensions
between parents and their children.
Bless, O Lord, all whose homes have fallen apart
and all children who have been taken into care.

David Adam

218 We give thanks
that you appeared in an ordinary home, O Christ.
We ask that your presence and your peace
may be known in our homes and among our loved ones.
We bring before you homes
where faith is mocked or persecuted,
and pray for all who are struggling to remain faithful.

David Adam

219 We give thanks because you show us your love
through those who love us.
We ask your blessing
upon our homes and our loved ones.
We pray for homes where there is stress and distress.
We remember all who are finding it difficult to cope
and those who are deeply in debt.
We pray for all who are seeking to help those in need.

David Adam

220 We give thanks for the great riches you have given us
through our home and loved ones.
May we always appreciate the care and attention
that have been shown to us.
As we have richly received, so may we share;
as we are loved, so may we love.
We pray for homes where there is tension
and a breakdown in relationships.   *David Adam*

221 We thank you for our homes and our loved ones.
We ask your blessing
upon those who are moving to a new home
or who are moving away from their families.
We remember all who are homeless,
all who live in poverty or hunger.
We pray to you for all who work
to relieve the needs and suffering of others.   *David Adam*

222 Lord, may our homes reflect the love we share.
Keep us sensitive to the needs of each other.
May we be ready to take our share
in the work of our own home.
We remember before you
all who feel unloved and unwanted.
We ask your blessing
upon all homeless people and refugees.
We pray for all who are suffering
from broken relationships and broken trust.   *David Adam*

223 Lord, may we be at home with you in our homes.
When our hearts burn within us,
may we know that you are near.
Help us to know you are with us
in all our dealings with others.
We remember today all who are lonely or feel rejected
and all who feel they are missing out on life.   *David Adam*

224 We give thanks for the love and protection of our parents.
We ask your blessing upon our homes
and all our loved ones,
that they may live in peace and be free from poverty.
We remember all children who have been taken into care
and all families who find it difficult to cope.
We pray for any parents who have lost a child
over this past year.   *David Adam*

225 We ask your blessing upon our homes and families.
We bring before you all who are suffering
from broken relationships and broken homes.
We pray for those who have been rejected
by their families
and all who feel they have been betrayed in love.
Bless all who work to bring reconciliation
and new hope to separated peoples.   *David Adam*

226 God of family and friendship,
may all that occurs in families
be blessed with an openness of spirit
and a wave of unconditional love.
Let us be open to challenges,
but always enfolded in the love which binds us,
and the love you have shown to us,
through your Son, Jesus Christ.   *Rupert Bristow*

227 Astonishing Lord,
who made heaven and earth,
and brought man and woman into the world,
to your delight and our eternal gratitude,
let us be worthy of your trust
and the second chance you have given us,
to give firm foundations to family members
and true friendship to neighbours,
as your Son taught us.   *Rupert Bristow*

228   Long-suffering Lord,
         bring us patience and perseverance
         in maintaining family relationships,
         turning disunity into harmony,
         jealousy or envy into trust.
         May we set an example to the next generation
         by promoting your values
         and worshipping your holy name,
         through Jesus Christ.   *Rupert Bristow*

229   Amazing God,
         you sent your Son as a member of the human family,
         to have and to hold,
         to worship and adore.
         Let us model your generosity
         in all our family dealings,
         as the father of the prodigal son showed us
         and the mother of your Son proved to us.   *Rupert Bristow*

230   Lord of relationship,
         make families secure;
         may each generation be grateful to the last;
         may family feuds turn into family friendships;
         may our hearts be gladdened at family achievements,
         but, above all:
         let us know your blessings,
         in our homes, in our households,
         and in our family celebrations,
         Father God.   *Rupert Bristow*